A World of Recipes

Greece

Sue Townsend

Heinemann
Library
Chicago, Illinois

© 2002 Reed Educational & Professional Publishing
Published by Heinemann Library,
an imprint of Reed Educational & Professional Publishing,
Chicago, Illinois

Customer Service 888-454-2279

Visit our website at www.heinemannlibrary.com

Designed by Tinstar Design
Illustrations by Nicholas Beresford-Davies
Originated by Dot Gradations
Printed by Wing King Tong in Hong Kong

06 05 04 03 02
10 9 8 7 6 5 4 3 2 1

Library of Congress Cataloging-in-Publication Data
Townsend, Sue, 1963-
    Greece / Sue Townsend.
       p. cm. -- (A world of recipes)
    Includes bibliographical references and index.
    Summary: A collection of recipes from Greece, plus cultural and
nutritional information.
    ISBN 1-58810-611-X
    1. Cookery, Greek--Juvenile literature. [1. Cookery, Greek.]   I.
Title. II. Series
    TX723.5.G8 T58 2002
    641.59495--dc21
                                    2001004808

Acknowledgments
The author and publishers are grateful to the following for permission to reproduce copyright material: p 5 Corbis; all other photographs Gareth Boden.

Cover photographs reproduced with permission of Gareth Boden.

Every effort has been made to contact copyright holders of any material reproduced in this book. Any omissions will be rectified in subsequent printings if notice is given to the publisher.

Some words are shown in bold, **like this.** You can find out what they mean by looking in the glossary.

Contents

Key

* easy

** medium

*** difficult

Greek Food

Greece is a Mediterranean country made up of a mainland and over 2,000 islands that are scattered throughout the Aegean and Ionian seas. However, only 151 of these islands have people living on them.

In the past

Several civilizations have lived in Greece at different times over the past 2,000 years. These include the ancient Greeks, the ancient Romans, and the Phoenicians, who were traders who sailed to the far East and brought back spices. Each civilization has cooked and prepared food differently.

Around the country

Summer in Greece is very hot, but the winters can be cold and rainy. The main crops of the country have always been wheat, olives, and grapes. Much of the land is mountainous, making farming difficult. Sheep and goats wander over the slopes, but only tough plants, such as thyme and rosemary, grow well there.

In more sheltered areas, farmers grow fruits and vegetables such as lemons and eggplants. They also grow almonds, pistachios, and walnuts. Many Greek people keep bees, using their honey to sweeten foods.

▲ *With over 9,000 miles (15,000 km) of shoreline, fishing is an important Greek industry.*

Because meat can be scarce, it is usually served with rice, lentils, and bread to make a small piece feed more people. Cooks use sheep and goat's milk to make milk, creamy yogurt, and cheese. Greek people often cook meat for special holidays, such as Easter. During festivals, a Greek family might roast a whole lamb.

Greek meals

In Greece, meals often begin with a selection of cooked vegetables and yogurt dishes, called a *mezze* (pronounced met-say). These might be followed by fish or meat that has been **marinated** in olive oil with herbs and vegetables, and then grilled or **baked.** Cooks often grill fish and meat with lemons, tomatoes, and spices. Common desserts include fruit, such as figs, melons, dates, and oranges, or yogurt and honey.

Ingredients

melons

eggplant

zucchini

peppers

romaine lettuce

parsley

feta cheese

lemons

olives

figs

garlic

grapes

tomatoes

almonds

pine nuts

herbs

cinnamon

dates

Eggplants

Greek cooks often stuff eggplants with a rice filling. They also **bake** them slowly, then blend them with olive oil, onions, and garlic to make a creamy dip. You can buy eggplants at most supermarkets.

Almonds

Almonds were first brought to Greece centuries ago by traders from Asia. They are used in many sweet and **savory** Greek recipes. **Peeling** off their brown skin is tricky, so buy skinless blanched ones if you can.

Feta

Feta is a cheese made from sheep or goat's milk. It is kept fresh in brine (salt water). If feta tastes too salty to you, soak it in cold water overnight before using it. You can buy feta cheese in most larger supermarkets.

Cumin and coriander

These two spices are often used together in savory Greek dishes. Neither is a hot spice. The seeds are usually lightly **fried** or toasted before they are added to dishes.

Herbs

Basil, dill, mint, oregano, parsley, rosemary, thyme, and bay leaves are all used to flavor Greek dishes. These herbs are available dried and fresh in supermarkets.

Olives

On the olive tree, olives start off yellow and turn green as they grow. Farmers pick them at this point, and leave them to ripen more in the sun until they turn purple, brown, and eventually black. Most Greek dishes use black olives. You can buy whole olives with the pit in them, or pitted olives with the pit taken out. They are available in jars and cans, or loose from the deli counter of most supermarkets.

Grape leaves

Grape leaves are the large leaves that grow on grapevines. They are commonly eaten in Greece stuffed with a rice or meat stuffing and formed into rolls. Grape leaves are usually packed in brine in jars, or preserved in plastic packages. Look for them at larger supermarkets.

Yogurt

Greek yogurt is very thick and creamy. It is usually made from sheep or goat's milk. It is very thick because it has cream added to it. It is available in larger supermarkets. If you can't find Greek yogurt, you can use plain, unflavored yogurt instead.

Before You Begin

Kitchen rules

There are a few basic rules you should always follow when you cook:

- Ask an adult if you can use the kitchen.
- Some cooking processes, especially those involving hot water or oil, can be dangerous. When you see this sign, take extra care or ask an adult to help.
- Wash your hands before you start.
- Wear an apron to protect your clothes. Tie back long hair.
- Be very careful when using sharp knives.
- Never leave pan handles sticking out—it could be dangerous if you bump into them.
- Always wear oven mitts when lifting things in and out of the oven.
- Wash fruits and vegetables before using them.

How long will it take?

Some of the recipes in this book are quick and easy, and some are more complicated and take longer. The strip across the top of the right-hand page of each recipe tells you how long it will take to cook each dish from start to finish. It also shows how difficult each dish is to make:

* (easy), ** (medium), or *** (difficult).

Quantities and measurements

You can see how many people each recipe will serve at the top of each right-hand page, too. Most of the recipes in this book make enough to feed two or four people. You can multiply or divide the quantities if you want to cook for more or fewer people.

Ingredients for recipes can be measured in two ways. Imperial measurements use cups and ounces. Metric measurements use grams and milliliters. In these recipes you will see the following abbreviations:

tbsp = tablespoon   oz = ounce
tsp = teaspoon   lb = pound
ml = milliliter   cm = centimeter
g = gram   mm = millimeter

Utensils

To cook the recipes in this book, you will need these utensils, as well as kitchen essentials such as spoons, plates, and bowls:

- baking sheet
- electric mixer
- food processor or blender
- large frying pan
- citrus juicer
- measuring cups
- measuring spoons
- cutting board
- small screw-topped jar
- saucepans with lids
- sharp knife
- ovenproof baking dishes
- square cake pan
- round cake pan
- metal skewers
- grill pan
- parchment paper
- pastry brush
- sieve

 Whenever you see this symbol, be very careful.

Eggplant and Lentil Soup

In Greece, many people grow eggplants in their gardens. Eggplants can have purple skin, white skin, or purple skin flecked with white. They are always cooked before they are eaten. Look for an eggplant that has firm, shiny skin. An eggplant with wrinked skin may taste bitter.

What you need

1 small eggplant
¼ cup (40 g) dried lentils
1 onion
1 clove garlic
1 tbsp oil
1 vegetable stock cube
3 tbsp **tahini**
salt and pepper

What you do

1 **Preheat** the oven to 350°F (180°C). Put the eggplant on a baking sheet and **bake** it for 30 minutes. Leave it to cool.

2 Meanwhile, put the lentils and 2 ½ cups (600 ml) cold water into a pan. Bring to a **boil.** Boil the lentils for ten minutes and then **simmer** them for ten more minutes until they are tender. **Drain** any extra water.

3 **Peel** and **chop** the onion and garlic.

4 Heat the oil in a frying pan, add the chopped onion, and **fry** it over low heat for three minutes.

5 Add the garlic and cook for two more minutes.

6 Cut the eggplant in half. Scoop out the flesh.

7 Spoon the lentils into a blender or food processor. Add the eggplant flesh, tahini, onion, and garlic. Crumble in the stock cube.

8 Blend the mixture until it is smooth. Carefully stir in 1 ¼ cups (300 ml) of hot water.

9 Pour the soup into a saucepan and simmer it for two minutes.

10 Add a little salt and pepper. Serve warm with pita bread (page 12).

Pita Bread

In Greece, pita bread is served with many meals and used to scoop up food. Pita bread is also often filled with salads and meats, like a sandwich.

What you need

3 cups (350 g) bread flour
½ tsp salt
1 ¼-oz (7-g) packet active dry yeast
2 tbsp olive oil

What you do

1 Put the flour, salt, oil, and yeast into a food processor. Put the lid on and process, pouring 1 cup (230 ml) of warm water slowly through the funnel until a soft dough forms.

2 Process for 3 more minutes. Put the dough into a bowl. Rub a little olive oil over a sheet of plastic wrap and cover the bowl with it. Allow the dough to rise in a warm place for about 40 minutes.

3 Cut the dough into eight pieces of equal size.

4 Roll out one piece of dough with a rolling pin until it makes a circle about 8 inches (20 cm) wide. Fold it in half and form it into a teardrop shape. Put it onto a baking sheet.

5 Repeat this for all pieces of dough. Cover them with oiled plastic wrap and leave them in a warm place for 30 minutes to rise again.

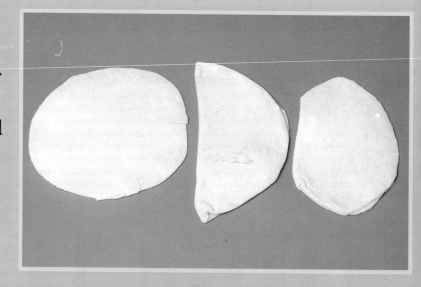

6 **Preheat** the oven to 450°F (220°C). Remove the plastic wrap and **bake** the pita bread for about eight minutes.

7 Sprinkle some water onto a clean kitchen towel and spread it over the pitas once they come out of the oven. This will keep some steam inside them as they cool and help keep them puffy.

8 Hold them with a clean kitchen towel to protect your hands from hot steam when you split them. Serve with main dishes or salads.

Tzaziki with Grilled Vegetables

Tzaziki (pronounced sat-ZEE-kee) is a sauce of **chopped** cucumber and yogurt. It sometimes also has chopped mint and garlic added to it. In Greece, it is served with pita bread or with a selection of other dishes, such as grilled vegetables.

Greek cooks would serve the grilled vegetables at room temperature, or chill them and serve them cold.

What you need

For the roasted vegetables:
1 red pepper
1 yellow pepper
1 zucchini
½ an eggplant
2 tbsp olive oil

For the tzaziki:
½ a cucumber
⅔ cup (150 ml) Greek-style or plain yogurt
1 clove garlic (optional)
salt and pepper

What you do

1 Cut the peppers into quarters. Cut out and throw away the stalks and seeds.

2 Lay the pepper pieces skin side up onto a grill pan or frying pan.

3 Cut the zucchini and eggplant into thin **slices**. Put them onto the grill pan or frying pan.

4 Brush the vegetables with some of the olive oil.

5 Cook the vegetables over medium heat until they start to turn brown on one side. Using a fork, turn the vegetables over. Brush with a little more oil and continue to cook them for a few minutes.

6 When the peppers' skins have turned black, put them into a small plastic container and put the lid on. Leave them to cool.

7 **Peel** off the peppers' skins.

8 Wash the cucumber and cut it into thin slices. Cut the slices into thin strips. Cut these into small cubes.

9 Put the cubes into a sieve and allow the juice to **drain** for five minutes.

10 Stir the cucumber into the yogurt. Peel and crush the garlic and stir into the sauce (if using garlic).

11 Add a little salt and pepper and spoon into a bowl. Serve with the grilled vegetables.

Horiatiki Salata

During the hot Greek summers, many people eat in outdoor restaurants called tavernas. Horiatiki salata, (pronounced HOR-ee-a-TEE-kee sa-LAH-ta) which means "country salad," is a popular dish in tavernas. It is often called "Greek salad" in the United States.

What you need

For the salad:
1 bunch romaine lettuce
½ a cucumber
2 tomatoes
1 small onion
6 oz (170 g) feta cheese
16 to 20 black olives

For the dressing:
6 tbsp olive oil
3 tbsp lemon juice

What you do

1 Cut the lettuce head in half lengthwise. Wash the leaves and gently pat them dry with a clean kitchen towel. Cut the lettuce into pieces.

2 Wash the cucumber and **slice** it. Cut each slice into quarters.

3 Wash the tomatoes and **chop** them into small pieces. **Peel** and slice the onion.

4 Cut the feta cheese into small cubes.

5 Put the chopped lettuce, cucumber, onion, and tomatoes into a serving bowl. Add the feta cheese and olives.

6 Put the oil and lemon juice into a small screw-topped jar. Just before serving the salad, shake the dressing well and pour it over the salad.

EATING OUTSIDE

Every town and village in Greece has at least one taverna. In the summer, diners enjoy their meals surrounded by trailing vines and pots of brightly colored flowers. Often musicians will play traditional Greek music while people eat.

Moussaka

Moussaka is one of the most famous Greek dishes. For a **vegetarian** version, start at step 3, replacing the meat with 1 lb (450 g) of chopped mushrooms and an extra eggplant.

What you need

1 lb (450 g) ground lamb
 (or beef if you prefer)
1 large onion
1 tbsp olive oil
2 cloves garlic
1 ½ tsp cumin
1 ½ tsp coriander
1 tsp dried thyme
1 zucchini
1 14.5-oz (425-g) can
 diced tomatoes
1 eggplant
1 potato

For the white sauce:
1 ¼ cup (300 ml) milk
3 tbsp cornstarch

What you do

1 Put the ground lamb into a saucepan and pour in enough cold water to cover it. Bring it to a **boil, cover** it and cook over medium heat for five minutes, stirring occasionally.

(!) 2 Put a sieve over a bowl and carefully pour the meat into it.

(!) 3 **Peel** and **slice** the onions. Heat the oil in a pan and **fry** them over low heat for five minutes.

4 Peel and crush the garlic. Add it to the pan along with the drained lamb meat, cumin, coriander, and thyme. Cook for three minutes, stirring occasionally.

5 Cut the ends off the zucchini. Cut the zucchini into small cubes. Add the zucchini and the tomatoes to the pan. Cover and **simmer** for 20 minutes.

6 **Preheat** the oven to 375°F (190°C).

7 Peel the potato and cut it into thin slices. Put the slices into a saucepan, cover them with water, and boil for five minutes. **Drain** the potato slices.

8 Cut both ends off the eggplant. Cut the eggplant into thin slices. Fry the slices in a nonstick frying pan, without any oil, over low heat for three minutes. Turn them over and cook the other side for three minutes.

9 In a small pan, stir a little of the milk into the cornstarch to make a smooth paste. Add the rest of the milk. Heat, stirring all the time, until the sauce thickens.

10 Spoon the meat mixture into a 1 ½ quart (1 ½ liter) ovenproof dish. Layer the eggplant and potato slices on top. Pour the sauce over the top of the whole thing.

11 **Bake** for 30 minutes. Serve with a salad.

Burekakia

Burekakia (pronounced boo-ra-KA-kee-ah) are **phyllo** pastry triangles filled with feta cheese and spinach. In Greece, people buy them hot from street vendors.

What you need

1 10-oz (280-g) package frozen spinach, **thawed** and **drained**
2 oz (55 g) feta cheese
½ tsp cinnamon
2 tbsp fresh mint, **chopped**
1 package frozen phyllo dough, thawed
4 tbsp butter
salt and pepper

What you need

1 Put the spinach into a sieve and press out any liquid with a spoon. Place it on a cutting board and chop it finely. Put it into a bowl.

2 Crumble the feta into the bowl and add the cinnamon, mint, and a little salt and pepper. Stir well.

3 Lay the phyllo pastry on a cutting board. Cut it into three 4-inch (10-cm) by 20-inch (50-cm) strips. Divide the layers of each strip to form three strips with the same number of dough layers. Cut each of these nine strips in half so that you have 18 strips that are 10 inches (25 cm) long. Cover them with plastic wrap to keep them from drying out.

4 Put the butter into a small saucepan. Heat it gently until it melts.

5 Line a baking sheet with parchment paper.

6 Brush one strip of pastry with melted butter. Place a heaping teaspoonful of the spinach and feta mixture about 1 inch (3 cm) from the top.

7 Fold the right-hand top corner over the filling and across to the left-hand edge to form a triangle, as shown.

8 Fold the triangle down over the pastry immediately below it to form a straight edge along the top again. Continue folding down the length of the phyllo strip. Brush the finished triangle with butter and place it on the baking sheet.

9 Repeat steps 6 to 8 until all of the pastry strips are used.

10 **Preheat** the oven to 400°F (200°C). **Bake** the burekakia for ten to twelve minutes, or until golden brown. Serve them hot or cold.

Popolettes

Greek cooks often use leftover boiled potatoes to make these little potato patties filled with onion, feta cheese, and dill.

What you need

2 potatoes
2 oz (55 g) feta cheese
2 green onions
2 tbsp fresh dill, **chopped**
½ tsp fennel seeds
2 tbsp olive oil

What you do

1 Peel the potatoes and chop them into 1-inch (3-cm) cubes. Put the cubes into a saucepan and cover them with water.

(!) **2** Add a pinch of salt and bring to a **boil.** Cook the potatoes for ten minutes. **Drain** and **mash** them.

3 Crumble the feta cheese into a bowl. Cut the roots and tops off of the green onions. Chop the onions finely and add them to the feta.

4 Stir in the dill, fennel seeds, and mashed potato.

5 On a cutting board, shape the mixture into six patties.

(!) **6** Heat the oil in a frying pan. **Fry** the patties over medium heat for three minutes. Using a spatula, turn them over and cook the other side.

7 Serve the popolettes hot or cold with grilled meat, fish, or vegetables.

CRACKED POTATOES

Here is another way Greek cooks serve potatoes. They cook new potatoes until they are tender, then they drain them and add chopped tomatoes, olive oil, a few mustard seeds, and some chopped parsley to the pan. After putting the pan lid on, they shake the potatoes until the peels break open and the tomato juice soaks into them.

Stuffed Peppers and Tomatoes

In Greece, many people grow peppers and tomatoes in their gardens, where vegetables ripen quickly in the hot sun. There are many variations on this dish in different areas of the country.

What you need

½ cup (100 g) uncooked long-grain rice
1 red pepper
1 yellow pepper
4 small tomatoes
1 onion
2 cloves garlic
1 tbsp olive oil
½ tsp cumin
½ tsp dried thyme
¼ cup (30 g) raisins

What you do

1 Put the rice into a saucepan with 1 ¼ cup (300 ml) hot water. **Cover** the pan and bring to a **boil. Simmer** for fifteen minutes, until the rice is tender.

2 **Preheat** the oven to 375°F (190°C). Cut the peppers in half through the stalk. Using a spoon, scoop out the seeds.

3 Cut the tomatoes into halves. Scoop out the insides. Put the insides into a bowl and **chop** them up.

4 Put the pepper and tomato halves onto a baking sheet.

5 **Peel** the onion and the garlic, and chop finely.

6 Heat the oil in a saucepan and **fry** the chopped onion for three minutes. Add the garlic, cumin, and thyme and cook for one minute.

7 Stir in the chopped tomato and raisins. Cook for two minutes, then stir in the cooked rice. Spoon the hot mixture into the pepper and tomato shells.

8 **Bake** for 20 minutes. Using a spatula, carefully lift the peppers and tomatoes off the baking sheet onto plates.

9 Serve as a **vegetarian** main dish, or as a side dish with meat or fish.

Lamb Kebabs

Many sheep graze on the mountainous slopes of Greece, so lamb is easily available. If you prefer, replace the lamb with boneless, skinless chicken breast in this recipe. Try cooking your kebabs on a barbecue, as many Greek cooks would.

What you need

2 lbs (900 g) lean lamb
1 onion
1 tsp dried oregano
sprigs of fresh rosemary
1 lemon
½ cup (120 ml)
   olive oil
salt and pepper
lemon wedges
   to **garnish**

What you do

1 Cut off as much fat as you can from the lamb. Cut the lamb into bite-size cubes and put them in a bowl.

2 **Peel** and **chop** the onion. Add the onion, oregano, and rosemary to the lamb.

3 Cut the lemon in half. Using a citrus juicer, squeeze out the juice. Chop the lemon peel into small pieces.

4 Add the olive oil, lemon peel, lemon juice, and a little salt and pepper to the lamb. Stir well, **cover**, and chill for at least four hours, or overnight if possible. During this time, the meat soaks up the flavors of the **marinade**.

5 Take the lamb out of the bowl. Thread the cubes onto four metal skewers.

6 **Broil** in the oven for about ten minutes, using oven mitts to turn the skewers so that the meat browns evenly. Cut a piece of meat in half to check that it is cooked. It should be slightly pink or a pale brown color in the middle.

7 Garnish with rosemary and lemon wedges, if you like, and serve with a salad and pita bread.

Fish with Red Pepper and Tomato Sauce

Because Greece has such a long shoreline, fish and seafood are plentiful and are served in a variety of ways. In the many coastal villages, fresh fish is sold on beds of ice outside tavernas and freshly caught octopus, which is a popular food, is hung out to dry.

What you need

1 red pepper
1 onion
2 cloves garlic
3 tbsp olive oil
1 14.5-oz (425-g) can diced tomatoes
1 lb (450 g) firm white fish (such as cod or whitefish)

What you do

1 Cut the pepper in half and remove the stalk and seeds. Cut the pepper into quarters.

2 **Broil** the pepper skin side up until the skin starts to blacken. Put the pepper pieces into a plastic container with a lid. Put the lid on, leave the pepper to cool, then **peel** off the skin.

3 Turn the oven to 400°F (200°C). Peel and **chop** the onion and garlic.

4 Heat the oil in a saucepan and cook the chopped onion over a low heat for five minutes. Add the garlic and cook for two more minutes.

5 Stir in the tomatoes and peeled red pepper, and cook for five minutes. Cool slightly, then spoon the mixture into a blender or food processor. Put the lid on and process until smooth.

6 Cut the fish into two portions. Wipe a little oil onto the bottom of an ovenproof dish. Lay the fish in it, pour the sauce over, and cover the dish.

7 Cook in the oven for fifteen minutes or until the fish is very white and firm. **Garnish** with parsley and serve with a salad.

Stuffed Grape Leaves

In Greece, cooks stuff fresh grape leaves with various ingredients, including spicy ground meat and rice mixtures. In this **vegetarian** version of the dish, the grape leaves are stuffed with rice, herbs, pine nuts, and raisins. Fresh grape leaves are hard to find in the United States, but most supermarkets sell jars or packets of preserved grape leaves.

What you need

1 jar or packet preserved grape leaves
1 onion
2 cloves garlic
2 tbsp olive oil
¾ cup (150 g) uncooked long-grain rice
¼ cup (40 g) pine nuts
¼ cup (40 g) raisins
2 tsp fennel seeds
2 tbsp fresh mint, **chopped**
4 tbsp fresh parsley, chopped

What you do

1 Put the grape leaves in cold water to soak. **Peel** and finely chop the onion and garlic.

2 Heat the oil in a small saucepan and **fry** the onion and garlic over low heat for three minutes.

3 Put the onions and garlic into a bowl. Stir in the uncooked rice, pine nuts, raisins, fennel seeds, mint, and parsley.

4 Lay a grape leaf on a cutting board, with the veined side facing up. Cut off the stalk if it sticks out. Put a heaping teaspoonful of the mixture at the stalk end of the leaf.

5 Fold the stalk end of the grape leaf over the filling. Fold the sides in and roll up the leaf as tightly as you can.

6 Place the rolled leaf in a large saucepan or deep-sided frying pan with the loose side of the roll facing down.

7 Repeat steps 4 to 6 until the the pan bottom is covered with stuffed grape leaves.

8 Cover the rolls with water. Put a plate on top to press down on them. **Cover** the pan and **simmer** for 30 minutes. (Add extra water if the leaves start sticking to the pan.)

9 Carefully lift the stuffed grape leaves onto a plate. Serve hot or cold with a little yogurt for dipping.

Spiced Rice and Lentils

In Greece, rice and lentils are often cooked together with spices. This dish can be served on its own or as a side dish with grilled meat and a salad.

What you need

½ cup (100 g) dried lentils
2 small onions
2 tbsp vegetable oil
1 tsp cinnamon
½ tsp caraway seeds
½ cup (100 g) uncooked long-grain rice
1 14.5-oz (425-g) can diced tomatoes
2 tbsp fresh parsley, **chopped**

What you do

1 Put the lentils into a sieve and rinse them under cold, running water. Put them into a pot and cover them with water.

2 Bring the water to a **boil.** Boil the lentils for ten minutes, then **cover** and **simmer** for 20 minutes. Add some more hot water if the lentils start sticking to the pan.

(!) 3 **Drain** the lentils and set them aside.

4 **Peel** both onions. **Slice** one and finely chop the other.

(!) 5 Heat half of the oil in a large saucepan. **Fry** the chopped onion gently for five minutes.

6 Add the cinnamon, caraway seeds, and drained lentils to the pan. Stir in the rice, tomatoes, and ¾ cup (175 ml) hot water. Bring to a boil, cover, and simmer for 20 minutes.

⊘ 7 Heat the rest of the oil in a frying pan. Fry the sliced onion until it is browned and crispy.

8 Stir the chopped parsley into the rice and lentil mixture. Put onto a serving dish and **garnish** with the fried onion and more parsley.

Chicken with Lemons and Olives

The yards of many Greek homes have lemon trees growing in them. Greek cooks use lemons in both sweet and **savory** dishes. Lemon leaves are even used to line casserole dishes to keep the food in them from burning.

What you need

4 chicken leg or
   breast portions
½ tsp cinnamon
2 onions
3 tbsp olive oil
1 chicken stock cube
1 lemon
16 to 20 black olives
salt and pepper
sprigs of fresh thyme

What you do

1 **Preheat** the oven to 375°F (190°C). Cut off any fat or loose skin from the chicken portions.

2 Sprinkle the cinnamon and some salt and pepper over the skin.

3 **Peel** and **slice** the onions.

4 Heat the oil in a frying pan over medium heat. Add the chicken and sliced onion. **Fry** until the chicken is lightly browned all over.

5 Put the chicken and onion into an ovenproof dish. Crumble the stock cube into 1 ¼ cup (300 ml) hot water. Carefully pour the stock over the chicken.

6 Cut the lemon into wedges and add the lemon and thyme to the chicken. **Cover** the dish and **bake** for 30 minutes.

(!) 7 Carefully take the dish out of the oven. Stir in the olives, cover, and cook for 30 more minutes.

8 **Garnish** with a few sprigs of thyme. Serve hot.

LEMON SOUP

Lemons and chicken are paired in another classic Greek dish—a soup called *avgolemono* (pronounced AHV-go-LEM-on-oh), which is a creamy chicken and rice soup flavored with lemon.

Almond Cake

The pink blossom of almond trees is a familiar sight all over Greece. Almond cake is often cut into small squares and served with strong, Greek coffee in cafés.

What you need

2 eggs
½ cup (120 ml) olive oil
½ cup (120 ml) Greek-style or plain yogurt
3 tbsp honey
½ cup (100 g) sugar
2 tsp baking powder
¾ cup (100 g) flour
¾ cup (100 g) ground almonds
2 tbsp slivered almonds

What you need

1 **Preheat** the oven to 375°F (190°C). Line the base and sides of an 8-inch (20-cm) round cake pan with parchment paper.

2 To separate the egg yolks from the whites, crack an egg open carefully. Pass the yolk between the halves of the eggshell over a bowl until the white has dripped out into the bowl. Put the yolk into a separate bowl. Repeat for the second egg.

3 Put the olive oil, yogurt, and honey into a large bowl. Add the two egg yolks and **beat** the mixture until it is smooth.

4 Using an electric mixer or a **whisk**, whisk the egg whites until they are stiff.

5 Mix the sugar, baking powder, flour, and ground almonds together. Pour the dry mixture into the olive oil mixture.

6 Using a large metal spoon, gently cut through the mixture to **fold** in the dry ingredients.

7 Add the egg whites and fold them into the mixture with the metal spoon.

8 Spoon the batter into the cake pan. Smooth the top with the back of a spoon.

9 Scatter the slivered almonds over the cake.

10 **Bake** on the middle rack of the oven for 35 to 45 minutes, until the cake springs back when lightly pressed in the center.

11 Let the almond cake cool in the pan for ten minutes, then turn it out onto a wire cooling rack. Cut into slices and serve.

Greek Yogurt with Honey and Fruit

Honey is an important ingredient in Greek cooking. In Greece, fresh fruits such as figs, dates, and melons are often served with honey and yogurt as a simple dessert. The ancient Greeks believed that honey had special healing powers and spread it onto cuts and burns. Here, it is used just for its smooth, sweet taste.

What you need

⅔ cup (150 g) Greek-style or plain yogurt
3 tbsp honey
2 figs or 6 dates
2 large slices watermelon

What you do

1 Stir the yogurt and honey together gently until the honey is streaked throughout the yogurt. This is called a marbled effect.

2 Clean the figs and cut them into quarters. If you are using dates, cut them in half and remove the pits.

3 Lay the watermelon flat on a cutting board. Cut the hard green rind off.

4 Arrange the fruit onto two plates. Put a large spoonful of the yogurt and honey mixture onto each plate. Serve chilled.

GREEK HONEY

Bees collect pollen from flowers and take it back to their hives to make honey. The flavor of the honey depends on what kind of flowers the bees visited. Greek honey is dark and runny with a rich flavor. A very good kind of Greek honey comes from the capital city of Athens. It is called hymettus honey.

Baklava

Baklava is a traditional Greek pastry that is rich with honey and nuts. In Greece, people eat small pieces of it with with cups of strong coffee because it is so sweet.

What you need

1 package frozen **phyllo** dough, **thawed**
1 ¼ cup (200 g) shelled pistachios
¾ cup (150 g) blanched almonds
¼ cup (25 g) shelled walnuts
1 tsp cinnamon
¼ tsp cloves
4 tbsp butter
6 tbsp honey
½ cup (100 g) sugar
1 cinnamon stick

What you do

1 **Chop** the nuts in a food processor for a few seconds. Put them into a bowl. Add the ground cinnamon and cloves.

2 **Preheat** the oven to 350°F (180°C). Put the butter into a small saucepan and heat it gently until it has melted.

3 Using a pastry brush, brush one sheet of phyllo dough with melted butter, then fold it in half. Put the rest of the phyllo under plastic wrap to keep it from drying out.

4 Lay the pastry into an 8-inch (20-cm) square baking pan, letting any extra pastry hang over the sides. Repeat with another sheet of dough.

5 Scatter half of the nut mixture into the baking tray. Level the nuts with a spoon.

6 Cut the remaining phyllo dough into 8-inch (20-cm) squares. Brush three squares with butter and lay them on top of the nuts. Scatter the rest of the nuts over them.

7 Fold any excess dough over the nuts. Put any remaining pastry squares on top and brush with melted butter.

8 Cut the top of the baklava carefully into 1-inch (3-cm) squares, but don't let the knife cut all the way through to the baking pan.

9 **Bake** for 25 minutes. Meanwhile, put the honey, sugar, cinnamon stick, and ½ cup (120 ml) of water into a small pan. Heat gently until the sugar has dissolved.

⊘ 10 Pour the warm liquid over the hot baklava once it is out of the oven. Leave it to cool completely for an hour. Cut all the way through into squares and serve.

Lemonade

Lemons grow in many areas of Greece and are used in a variety of recipes. This is a popular drink, especially during the long, hot summers. Use unwaxed lemons if you can find them. Otherwise, scrub the lemon skins very well with warm water to remove any wax.

What you need

2 lemons
6 tbsp sugar

What you do

1 Using a vegetable peeler, **peel** the skin off of one lemon. (Try not to remove too much of the white part that is attached to the skin because it tastes bitter.) Put the peel into a large jug.

2 Cut both lemons in half. Using a citrus juicer, squeeze the juice from the lemons.

3 Put the lemon juice and sugar into the heatproof jug with the peel.

4 Measure 2 ¾ cup (650 ml) **boiling** water into a measuring cup and pour it over the peel into the jug. Stir well, cover with a clean kitchen towel, and leave to cool. When it has cooled off, chill the lemonade overnight in the refrigerator.

5 Put a sieve over a pitcher. Pour the lemonade through the sieve. Taste it and add a little extra sugar if you wish.

6 Pour into two glasses and add some sparkling water if you like. Serve chilled.

USING LEMONS

In addition to using them in lemonade, Greek cooks use lemons and lemon peel to add a tangy flavor to many dishes. They also use lemon juice to make meat more tender.

More Books

Cookbooks

Beatty, Theresa. *Food & Recipes of Greece*. New York: Rosen
 Publishing, 1999.

Loewen, Nancy. *Food in Greece*. Vero Beach, Fla.: Rourke
 Publications, 1991.

Villios, Lynn. *Cooking the Greek Way*. Minneapolis, Minn.:
 Lerner Publications, 2001.

Books about Greece

Adare, Sierra. *Greece the Culture*. New York: Crabtree
 Publishing, 1998.

Frank, Nicole and Hong Nam Yeoh. *Welcome to Greece*.
 Milwaukee, Wis.: Gareth Stevens, 2000.

Comparing Weights and Measures

3 teaspoons=1 tablespoon	1 tablespoon=½ fluid ounce	1 teaspoon=5 milliliters
4 tablespoons=¼ cup	1 cup=8 fluid ounces	1 tablespoon=15 milliliters
5 ⅓ tablespoons= ⅓ cup	1 cup=½ pint	1 cup=240 milliliters
8 tablespoons=½ cup	2 cups=1 pint	1 quart=1 liter
10 ⅔ tablespoons=⅔ cup	4 cups=1 quart	1 ounce=28 grams
12 tablespoons=¾ cup	2 pints=1 quart	1 pound=454 grams
16 tablespoons=1 cup	4 quarts=1 gallon	

Healthy Eating

This diagram shows which foods you should eat to stay healthy. You should eat 6 to 11 servings a day of foods from the bottom of the pyramid. Eat 2 to 4 servings of fruits and 3 to 5 servings of vegetables a day. You should also eat 2 to 3 servings from the milk group and 2 to 3 servings from the meat group. Do not eat too many foods from the top of the pyramid.

The Greek diet can be very healthy because it includes a lot of fresh fruits, vegetables, rice, grains, and fish. Meat is eaten less often in Greece. Most dishes use olive oil for cooking, which is healthier than other fats. Greek cakes and pastries are very sweet, so they should only be enjoyed once in a while.

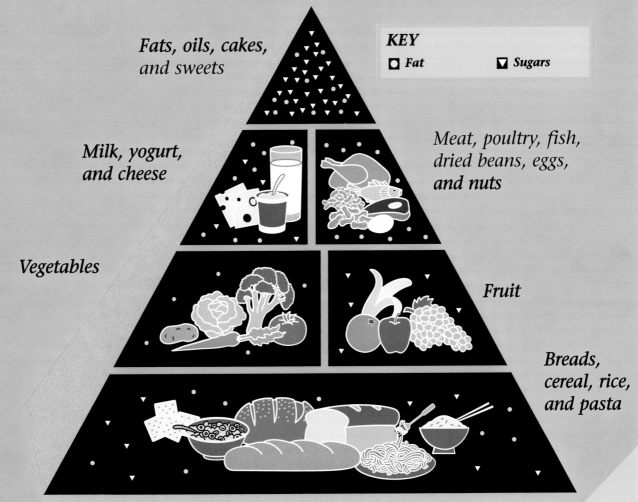

Fats, oils, cakes, and sweets

KEY
☐ Fat   ▽ Sugars

Milk, yogurt, and cheese

Meat, poultry, fish, dried beans, eggs, and nuts

Vegetables

Fruit

Breads, cereal, rice, and pasta

Glossary

bake to cook something in the oven

beat to mix something together strongly using a fork, spoon, or whisk

boil to heat liquid on the stove until it bubbles and steams strongly

broil to cook something under or over direct heat

chop to cut something into pieces with a knife

cover to put a lid on a pan or foil over a dish

drain to remove liquid from a pan or can of food

fold to gently mix ingredients together with a metal spoon using cutting movements to keep air in the mixture

fry to cook something in oil or butter in a pan

garnish to decorate food for serving, for example, with fresh herbs or lemon wedges

marinade sauce that food is left to soak in, so that the food absorbs the flavor of the sauce

mash to crush a food, such as potatoes or beans, until it is soft and smooth

peel to remove the outside of a fruit, vegetable, or hard-boiled egg

phyllo type of flaky pastry used in Greek cooking that is made of many layers of very thin dough

preheat to turn on the oven in advance, so that it is hot when you are ready to use it

savory not sweet

simmer to cook a liquid gently on the stove at just under a boil

slice to cut something into thin, flat pieces

tahini paste of ground sesame seeds

thaw to bring something that has been frozen to room temperature

vegetarian diet that usually does not include meat, poulty, or fish and that sometimes does not include eggs or dairy products. A person who follows such a diet is called a vegetarian.

whisk to beat air into ingredients by beating quickly with a utensil; the name of the wire utensil that is used for whisking together ingredients

Index